Designing Places and Spaces

Contents

Written by Adrian Bradbury

Collins

Design and designers

Every building you see around you, every car that passes you on the street, every stitch of clothing you wear, every game or toy you've ever played with, every sweet you've tasted, all have one thing in common. They all started out as the same thing: an idea.

The Mini Cooper was designed and built in the UK in 1961.

Houses of Parliament, London, UK, built 1840–70

The Rubik's Cube was designed by Hungarian Erno Rubik in 1980.

Someone, somewhere in the world had a new idea. They probably thought about it for a while, turning it over in their mind until they were happy with it. If they were very, very lucky, their idea would become so popular that they'd become rich and famous beyond their wildest dreams. But for most, a dream would be all that they were left with. For every idea that makes it into production, hundreds are never to be seen or even heard of.

Barbie turned 50 years old in 2009. She was designed by American Ruth Handler.

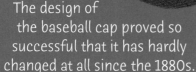

The design of the baseball cap proved so successful that it has hardly changed at all since the 1880s.

Cola Bottles are one of the world's best-selling sweets.

3

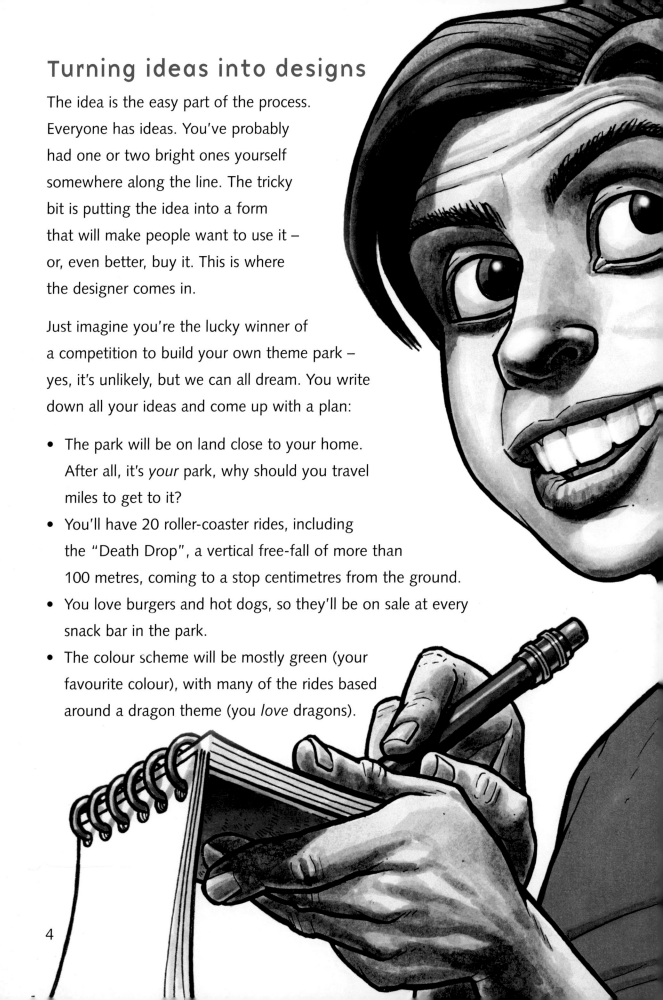

Turning ideas into designs

The idea is the easy part of the process. Everyone has ideas. You've probably had one or two bright ones yourself somewhere along the line. The tricky bit is putting the idea into a form that will make people want to use it – or, even better, buy it. This is where the designer comes in.

Just imagine you're the lucky winner of a competition to build your own theme park – yes, it's unlikely, but we can all dream. You write down all your ideas and come up with a plan:

- The park will be on land close to your home. After all, it's *your* park, why should you travel miles to get to it?
- You'll have 20 roller-coaster rides, including the "Death Drop", a vertical free-fall of more than 100 metres, coming to a stop centimetres from the ground.
- You love burgers and hot dogs, so they'll be on sale at every snack bar in the park.
- The colour scheme will be mostly green (your favourite colour), with many of the rides based around a dragon theme (you *love* dragons).

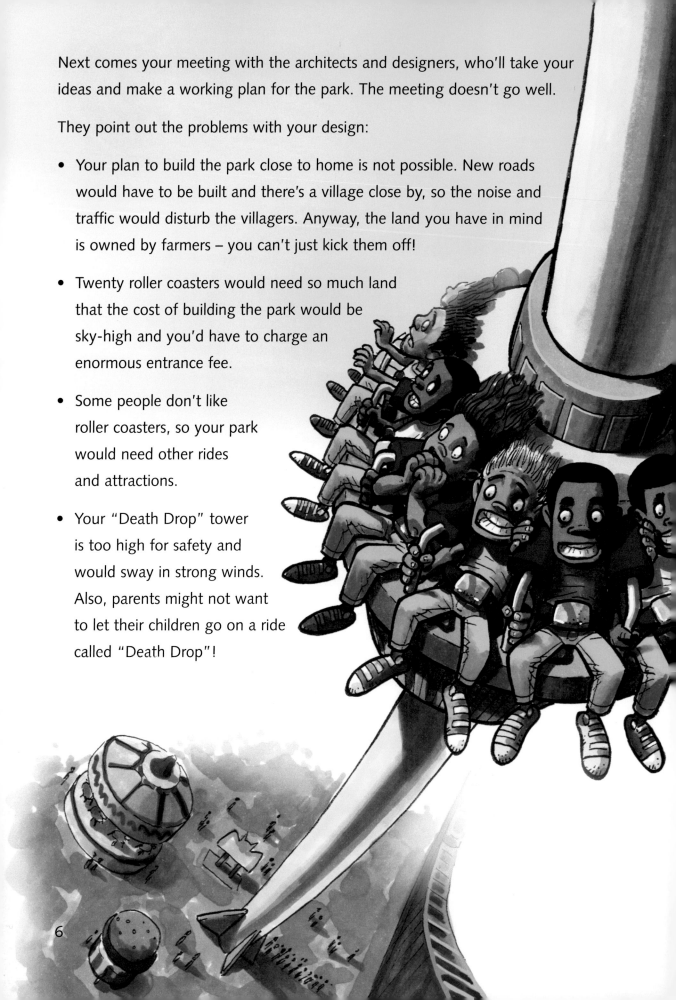

Next comes your meeting with the architects and designers, who'll take your ideas and make a working plan for the park. The meeting doesn't go well.

They point out the problems with your design:

- Your plan to build the park close to home is not possible. New roads would have to be built and there's a village close by, so the noise and traffic would disturb the villagers. Anyway, the land you have in mind is owned by farmers – you can't just kick them off!

- Twenty roller coasters would need so much land that the cost of building the park would be sky-high and you'd have to charge an enormous entrance fee.

- Some people don't like roller coasters, so your park would need other rides and attractions.

- Your "Death Drop" tower is too high for safety and would sway in strong winds. Also, parents might not want to let their children go on a ride called "Death Drop"!

- Your snack bars should include a variety of foods, such as salad, pasta, fruit or vegetarian dishes.

- Some might find the green colour scheme rather dull and research showed that some very young children were frightened by so many dragons.

- Your plans had no indoor attractions. What would happen when it rained? Would everyone go home?

- Your fences to stop children from sneaking in were high enough, but unfortunately you didn't have any emergency exits. Could everybody squeeze out through the main entrance? No.

Oh well. Nice try, young designer, but as you can see it's not an easy job! Let's take a look at how the experts design towns, buildings and spaces.

What does it take to make a building?

Now imagine you have enough money to build your dream home. This step-by-step guide shows you just what to do.

Step 1: The land

Once you've chosen and bought your land and got planning permission from the local council to build on it, you'll need a surveyor. He or she will make sure the ground is firm enough to support your house and check that there are no plans to build a motorway through your front garden in the near future!

Step 2: The design

You've probably got a rough idea of what you want and where you want it. Now you need an architect to design your house for you. He or she will take your ideas and come back with a plan and some drawings.

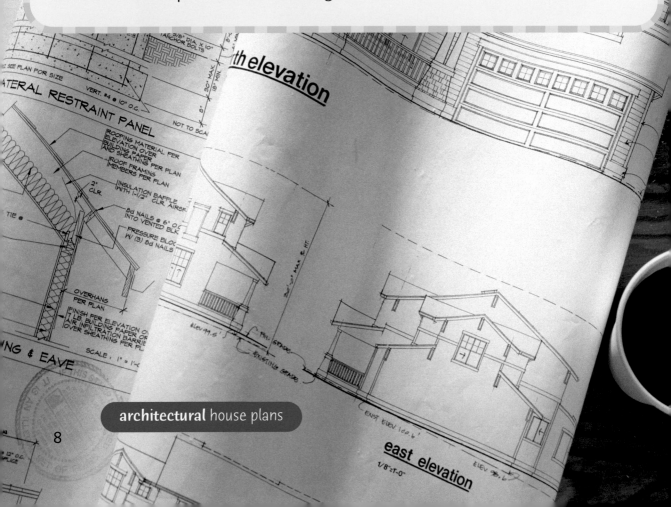

architectural house plans

After discussing them with you, the architect will draw up a more detailed design. There are lots of things to consider, such as:

- how the house will fit into the shape of your land
- which way the house should face to take advantage of views and sunlight
- how the house will look from the outside
- the layout of the rooms, making the best use of the available space
- the best place to put toilets and bathrooms
- the most suitable materials to use
- the best way to get water, electricity, gas and telephone lines to the house.

The architect may build a small model, or maybe produce a computer-generated tour of your virtual house and garden, to give you a true feel for how they will look.

An architect draws up a detailed plan of a house for the builder to follow.

Step 3: The building

1 Mechanical diggers will be brought in to make trenches so that all the drains and pipes can be put in the ground. Then they will flatten the land so that the **foundations** of your house can be put down.

2 Builders will put up the walls and the roof.

3 Plumbers will install the water and waste pipes.

4 Electricians will install the wiring between the walls and floors and in the roof.

5 **Insulation** will be crammed into the spaces in the walls, ceilings and roof to keep heat in.

6 Finally the doors, windows, flooring, fireplaces, lighting, plastering, painting, gutters, kitchen and bathroom furniture will be finished off. Fences will be put up around your land and turf will be laid in your garden.

Builders put up the walls and roof.

Plumbers install the water and waste pipes. Electricians install the electrical wiring.

The house is finished off. Turf is laid and fences put up around the garden.

Here are some famous architects, with some of the houses they designed.
Which house would you choose to live in? Would you like to make any changes to it?

Frank Lloyd Wright (1867–1959)
Many people have called him the greatest-ever American designer, not only of houses, but also of office blocks, churches, schools and hospitals.

Fallingwater House, built 1936–37, by Frank Lloyd Wright, is built over a waterfall so that house and nature blend together.

Hill House, built 1902–4, by Charles Rennie Mackintosh, is based on a traditional castle.

Charles Rennie Mackintosh
(1868–1928)
Mackintosh was a great Scottish architect and interior designer. He took the traditional style of castles and country houses, and mixed in his own, modern ideas.

Le Corbusier (1887–1965)
Le Corbusier was a French architect, furniture designer, town planner and painter. His designs were usually rectangular, with lengths and heights based on mathematical number patterns. They often contained sections supported by pillars or stilts.

Villa Savoye, built 1929–30, by Le Corbusier, is based on a mathematical number pattern.

Tall places and small spaces

As land in most city areas is extremely expensive, the cheapest way of getting yourself more space is to build upwards rather than sideways. This picture shows how the small, hilly area of Hong Kong has developed almost into a city in the sky.

Hong Kong skyline

By the 1850s engineers had already mastered the skill of building one floor on top of the other – the main problem was getting people from the bottom to the top. It was no use building a 20-storey office block if all the workers had to walk up and down the stairs every time they came in or out. Elevators, or "lifts", had been developed, but at the time they were unreliable and unsafe for very tall buildings.

The breakthrough arrived in 1853 when an American engineer, Elisha Otis, invented an automatic safety device that stopped a lift from falling even if the cable snapped.

Elisha Otis

Did you know?

Otis demonstrated his invention by riding up in an open-sided elevator, then asking his assistant to cut the cable! The elevator dropped only a few centimetres, to everyone's relief.

From that moment, the only way was up! New York's skyline changed constantly as taller and taller buildings sprang up. In 1928, car-company boss Walter Chrysler was able to boast that his new building was the tallest in the world at 319 metres. But his rival, General Motors boss John Raskob, cunningly topped this in 1931 by adding an airship mast to his own construction just a few blocks away, taking the Empire State Building to 381 metres. Tourists flocked to see the view from what was then the highest building in the world. Ever since, there has been a constant battle between cities and countries to claim the honour of the World's Tallest Building.

New York skyline

Empire State Building

Did you know?

- More than 21,000 people work in the Empire State Building every day.
- Seventy-three elevators are needed to cope with rush hour.
- In 1933 the fame of the building spread far and wide when it appeared in the film *King Kong*. The giant ape climbed to the top, with planes buzzing around his head, before falling to his death.

- The Empire State Run-Up is held every year to see who can be the fastest to race up the 1,576 steps from the ground floor to the observation deck on the 86th floor. The record is held by Australian Paul Crake, with a time of nine minutes and 33 seconds in 2003.

Chrysler Building

This diagram shows some of the titleholders for the world's tallest building over history.

2570 BC	1300	1889	1928	1931
Great Pyramid of Giza, Egypt	Lincoln Cathedral, UK	Eiffel Tower, Paris, France	Chrysler Building, New York, USA	Empire State Building, New York, USA
146 metres	160 metres	300 metres	319 metres	381 metres

1973	1998	2004	2009
Sears Tower, Chicago, USA	Petronas Towers, Kuala Lumpur, Malaysia	Taipei 101, Taiwan	Burj Dubai, United Arab Emirates
442 metres	452 metres	509 metres	estimated 818 metres

As technology has developed, engineers have been able to make buildings lighter, but also stronger and more stable. This has allowed architects to design buildings that look very different from the earliest brick and steel skyscrapers. Which of these do you find most beautiful?

the Chrysler Building, built 1928–30, New York, USA

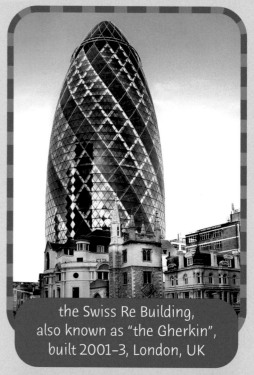

the Swiss Re Building, also known as "the Gherkin", built 2001–3, London, UK

the Burj Al Arab hotel, built 1994–99, Dubai, United Arab Emirates

Europe's most famous tall building is probably the Eiffel Tower in Paris. Designed by Gustave Eiffel and built for the World Fair in 1889, it attracts thousands of tourists every day, though originally it was intended to have only a 20-year lifespan before being pulled down.

Many Parisians felt that the beauty of their city's classical architecture was being spoilt by this iron giant. One famous writer, Guy de Maupassant, ate in its restaurant every day, because he said it was the only place in Paris where he couldn't see the Tower!

Did you know?

- The Eiffel Tower took 300 workmen two years to build.
- It's made of more than 7,000 tons of iron, and 60 tons of paint are needed to repaint it every seven years.
- More people have paid to visit the Eiffel Tower than any other building in the world – well over 200 million!
- Although it's very tall, the Eiffel Tower is not a skyscraper – skyscrapers need to have people living or working in them. So it's just a tower.

At home

Humans have always tried to build houses to fit their environment and way of life, using materials that are near at hand.

Inuit people in the Arctic built their igloos from blocks of ice. They were made small and solid because of the high winds.

Inuits building an igloo

American Indians used to build large tents called tepees, made from buffalo skins arranged around a structure of tree branches. The Indians led a **nomadic** life and tepees could be taken down and packed away quickly when it was time to move on.

an American Indian tepee

In South-East Asia, people find it difficult to clear a space in the dense woodland by the banks of a river, so they build houses on stilts driven into the river bed. These are close to their source of water, food and transport, as well as having some protection from flooding and from creatures living in the forest.

South-East Asian houses built on stilts in the river bed

In the UK there have been many changes in housing since the 1800s.

1850–1940 Poorer workers had to live near their work, so great blocks of cheap housing were built close to factories, mills and mines: row upon row of small houses, known as terraces, each one identical to the next. A tiny back yard was their outdoor space, but this would also contain their only toilet. Not a pleasant experience on those freezing winter mornings! Sometimes several families would live in the same house. Hygiene was very basic and disease could spread quickly.

terraced housing in **Victorian** England

People who could afford transport wanted to live further away from the crowds. Land was cheaper on the edges of towns and cities, so bigger houses could be built with large gardens to relax in. More and more people escaped the city centre to the **suburbs** in this way.

1940s   Many houses were destroyed in the Second World War (1939–45), so designers looked for a cheap way of rehousing as many families as possible in the shortest time. They came up with the "prefab" (short for "prefabricated"), a ready-built house like today's portakabins, that could be dropped into place and set up in as little as three hours. Prefabs were an instant hit for several reasons: they had electricity and running water readily available, often contained a garden for growing vegetables … and they had an inside toilet!

a prefab being built

a family ready to move into a completed prefab

1960–80 Blocks of flats started to appear in major cities – as land there was so expensive, it made sense to buy a small site and build upwards on it. At the time, it was thought that people would bond to form mini-communities within each block. Some people love living in tower blocks and enjoy the great views, but others may feel hemmed in if the lifts break down, or that there are not enough play areas for children. Many tower blocks were pulled down within 30 years and ways are being found to improve those that still exist, such as adding play areas for children. Nowadays, town planners prefer to design **low-rise** communities for families to live in.

Did you know?

The Government has tried to protect the countryside, stopping cities spreading too far by introducing Green Belts. These are areas around the edge of cities where you're not allowed to build.

Trellick Tower, London, UK, was completed in 1972 and has become a local landmark.

Inside the home

Designers have also faced the challenge of keeping up with fashions inside our homes. The 21st-century kitchen would be a place of mystery to a 1950s family. **Hi-tech** fridges and freezers mean that food can be bought in advance and then stored for weeks. Whole meals come in one frozen container, then ten minutes in a microwave oven and they're ready to eat. There's no need for a garden to hang the washing out, just press a button on the washer-dryer and it's taken care of.

a 1950s kitchen

a modern kitchen

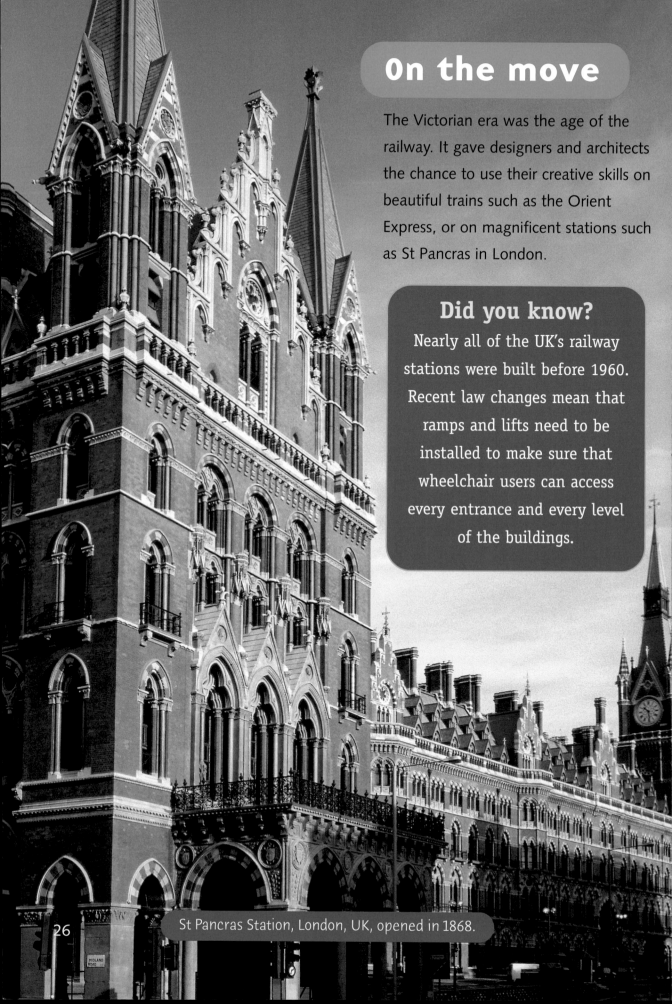

On the move

The Victorian era was the age of the railway. It gave designers and architects the chance to use their creative skills on beautiful trains such as the Orient Express, or on magnificent stations such as St Pancras in London.

Did you know?

Nearly all of the UK's railway stations were built before 1960. Recent law changes mean that ramps and lifts need to be installed to make sure that wheelchair users can access every entrance and every level of the buildings.

St Pancras Station, London, UK, opened in 1868.

However, most major developments in transport design had to wait until the 20th century and the increase in travel by road.

As the country began to get back to normal following the hardships of the Second World War, many more families found they were able to afford a car. It also became cheaper to transport goods by lorry rather than by train. The road network needed to develop to keep up. Wider roads were built, with three lanes of traffic and no junctions, traffic lights or roundabouts to slow things down – the motorway was born. Designers looked for ways to make motorways more functional and bridges more attractive.

the Gravelly Hill Interchange, Birmingham, UK, more usually known as "Spaghetti Junction"

As people spent more and more time in their cars, designers realised that they needed to make them more comfortable and include more features. A modern car is almost like a house on wheels. It has:

- soft, comfortable seats to sink into
- air conditioning to keep you at just the right temperature
- a high-quality sound system on which to play your CDs or plug your iPod into
- a **sat nav** system so that the driver need never get lost – he or she just has to put the address into the sat nav, then follow the directions given by the machine.

These three cars were on the roads in the mid-1960s. They're all now thought of as classic designs, but it's not too difficult to see which one was chosen as the car of choice for secret agent 007 James Bond.

The Fiat Cinquecento (Fiat 500) was the Italian version of the Mini and was first produced in 1957.

The Morris Minor was designed by Alex Issigonis (who also designed the Mini), in 1948.

The Aston Martin DB5 appeared in four James Bond films. It was manufactured between 1963–65.

The growth of the car brought with it other challenges for designers. With land so expensive in city centres, a new type of car park was needed that took up much less space but could hold more cars. The answer? Stack cars on top of each other.

This multi-storey car park in Gateshead, UK, was opened in 1969. Its design has caused many arguments over the years. The town planners would like to demolish it, but some locals love it and insist that it should be saved. The café you can see on the top floor has never opened.

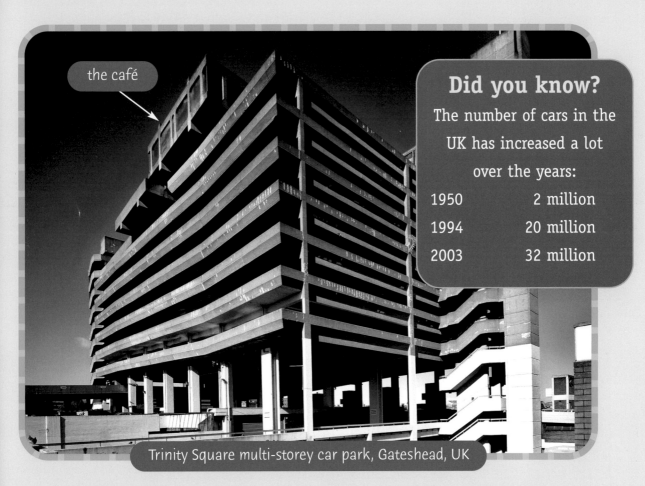

the café

Did you know?
The number of cars in the UK has increased a lot over the years:

1950	2 million
1994	20 million
2003	32 million

Trinity Square multi-storey car park, Gateshead, UK

One disadvantage of the increase in motor vehicles is that many cities are now clogged up with traffic, bringing pollution, delays, accidents and even **road rage**. The Government is trying to find ways of getting people to leave their beloved cars at home and take the bus instead.

In London a Congestion Charge was introduced in 2003 – drivers now have to pay to take their car into the city centre during the week.

Time for play

There has always been a strong link between design and the way we live our lives. Each one affects the other: new inventions such as mobile phones and e-mail have changed the way we communicate. In the same way, changes in the way we live mean designers need to come up with new ideas to fit our new lifestyle. This can be seen in the way we spend our free time.

1800s   As sports became more popular, architects were asked to build new stadiums to cope with the larger crowds. Many of these were later rebuilt to make them more comfortable, easier to get to, or safer (most of the first stadiums were built from wood, so they posed serious fire risks).

Villa Park football stadium, Birmingham, UK, 1907

In the evenings people flocked to the music halls to enjoy a laugh or sing along with the entertainers on stage. The most popular music halls were beautiful theatres, both inside and out.

1927 The first "talking picture", *The Jazz Singer*, was produced and cinema gradually took over from the music halls. Saturday afternoon matinée shows were packed out by children eagerly waiting for the latest adventure movie.

Did you know?

Some cinema audiences were entertained by huge Wurlitzer organs which rose majestically through a trapdoor in the floor!

a Saturday afternoon matinée cinema show, 1954

1930s   Cheaper radios and **gramophones** meant that people could now listen to their favourite music in the comfort of their own home.

In the USA the first drive-in cinemas opened, allowing the audience to enjoy the film without leaving their cars, while waitresses served food and drink.

an early drive-in cinema

1950s/60s More and more households could now afford a black and white television. The first programmes broadcast in colour in 1967 meant that cinemas became less popular.

The increase in overseas holiday travel resulted in a rise in the number of hotels worldwide. Large chains such as Holiday Inn and SAS made sure that all their hotels had the same design and colour schemes. The Danish architect Arne Jacobsen designed every aspect of the first SAS hotel in Copenhagen, including the famous "Egg" and "Swan" chairs.

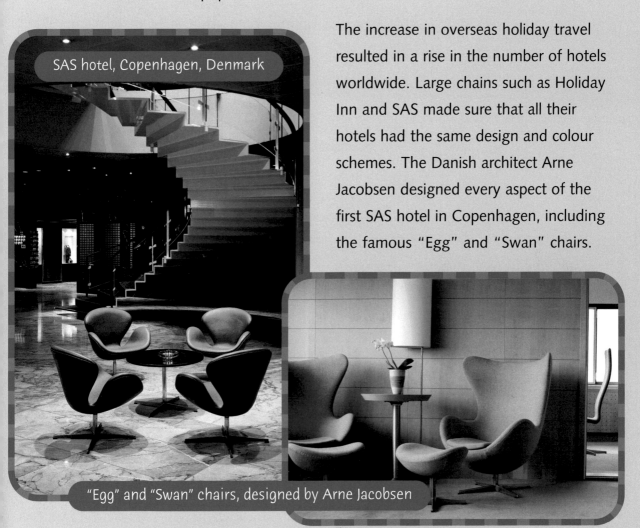

SAS hotel, Copenhagen, Denmark

"Egg" and "Swan" chairs, designed by Arne Jacobsen

1980s The invention of video recorders meant that parents had two options: pay for cinema tickets for a family, as well as transport, popcorn and drinks, or stay at home and rent a video from the nearest shop for much less money. Going out to the cinema became far less popular as people opted to stay at home and so they began to close down. However, the cinema industry fought back and modern "multiplexes" were designed. These contained ten or more small cinemas under one roof, showing a variety of different films and attracting a wider range of people. Going to the cinema became popular again.

1990s–present day   Digital satellite TV has made it even easier to avoid leaving the home for your entertainment, as the push of a button gives instant access to 50 or more channels.

Meanwhile, the development of computers has led to a huge change in the way we spend our leisure time. Many children now enjoy playing on the computer, but experts say that this trend is already having an effect on health and fitness.

Modern, tubular metal sports stadiums have replaced older designs. Some even feature a roof that can be closed to make sure events are not affected by bad weather.

Wembley Stadium, London, UK, built 2003–7

If you're travelling and just want a room to spend the night in, new "pod" hotels are now a cheap option. Putting your credit card into a slot unlocks the door to a tiny room with bed, TV and washing facilities, so no need for any staff.

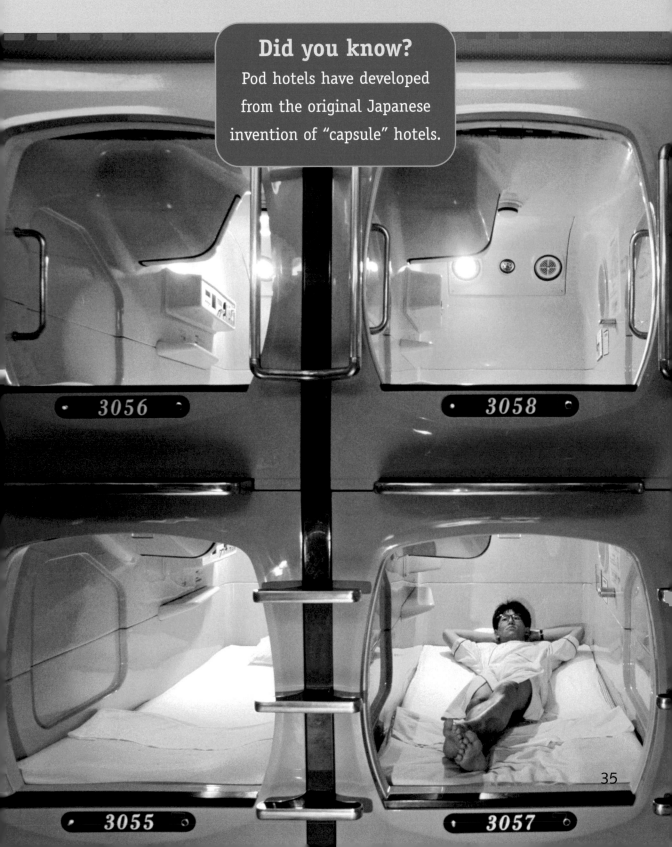

Did you know?
Pod hotels have developed from the original Japanese invention of "capsule" hotels.

3056

3058

3055

3057

Open spaces

People who design the layout of towns and cities are called Town Planners. One of the things they need to put into their plans is space for people to relax and play. On the edges of towns, where land is cheaper, this isn't such a problem, as houses can be built with large gardens. Inside the city, where buildings have crowded in upon each other and then grown upwards into the sky, gardens are rare, so precious land is reserved for parks. Even in the 1800s rich factory owners realised that their workers needed space in which to relax, as relaxing made them happier, and happier people usually work better.

map of London's parks

Regent's Park

Kensington Gardens

Hyde Park

Gunnersbury Park

Green Park

Battersea Park

Syon Park

London Wetland Centre

Bishop's Park

Kew Gardens

Barnes Common

Fulham Palace Gardens

Hurlingham Park

Clapham Common

Richmond Park

Wimbledon Common

Some parks are just open spaces of grassland sitting amongst the buildings – areas for people to stroll, play a game of football, maybe take a picnic, or just sit on a bench and enjoy some peace and quiet. The planner will probably include trees, plants and flowers to attract wildlife and make the park more beautiful.

Other parks are planned more as places of entertainment. Many of the first parks contained a boating lake. These were very popular with families, who could take to the water and imagine for a while that they were in the countryside or by the sea. Bandstands were built so that people could sit in the sunshine and listen to live music from the local brass band. There might even be an area in which to dance and have tea, and sometimes there were pools for children to paddle or swim in.

Parks of the world

In winter you can skate on the frozen lake in Central Park, New York, with skyscrapers towering over your head on all sides.

Even in the incredibly cramped spaces of downtown Hong Kong, parks play an important role in city life.

The largest city park in the world is Fairmount Park in Philadelphia, USA. Try to imagine 5,000 football pitches – that's how big it is!

The Carillon Belltower in Berlin's Tiergarten (Animal Park) has 68 bells. You can hear a concert every afternoon in the summer.

Phoenix Park in Dublin is the home of these deer, and the residency of the President of Ireland.

In Spain, a rich man, Count Güell, took the park idea a step further. He asked the famous architect Antoni Gaudí to build him a luxury private estate for rich people, on a bare hillside just outside the city of Barcelona. Gaudí planned a village within a magnificent park, which was to have its own church, market and sports arena. He brought in exotic plants from all around the world, and both the park and its buildings were decorated with weird and wonderful statues of brightly coloured mosaic. Unfortunately, the original idea wasn't a success. Only three houses were ever built there, and those included one for Count Güell and one for Gaudí!

Antoni Gaudí

view over Barcelona from Park Güell

Today, Park Güell is open to the public, and each summer thousands of tourists walk its winding paths, gazing in wonder at the amazing plants and bizarre buildings.

Park Güell

the Dragon Fountain, Park Güell

During the Second World War many towns were destroyed by bombs, so planners had the chance to redesign them entirely. They understood the need for open space, so each housing estate had small areas of grass to break up the buildings. Children weren't supposed to play on these and signs were put on posts, usually saying "Ball Games Prohibited". Children disagreed, often using the signposts as football goalposts or cricket wickets!

This boy had nowhere to kick his football.

Children were actually meant to play in small, fenced-off playgrounds, containing swings, a slide, climbing frame, roundabout and seesaw. This design has been a great success – you might have a very similar play area near your house today. The equipment may be a little more hi-tech and brightly coloured, with rubber surfaces underneath to prevent serious injury, but otherwise the design has stood the test of time.

a children's playground in Otley, Yorkshire, UK

As well as parks, some cities contain a large open square that might originally have been used for several purposes: grand parades, meetings, exhibitions, performances or maybe a bus station. Nowadays, these squares may appear to be a waste of valuable land, but they still have their uses. It's important for people to feel the freedom that empty space gives, especially when surrounded by so many high-rise buildings.

la Plaza Mayor, Madrid, Spain

43

Art in architecture

Some architects and designers believe that buildings shouldn't just be places in which to live or work, but should also be works of art to be admired. If we look back through history we can see that many of the world's most famous buildings are also amongst the most impressive or beautiful: the pyramids of ancient Egypt, the Colosseum of Rome, the Taj Mahal in India, the Leaning Tower of Pisa in Italy or London's Crystal Palace.

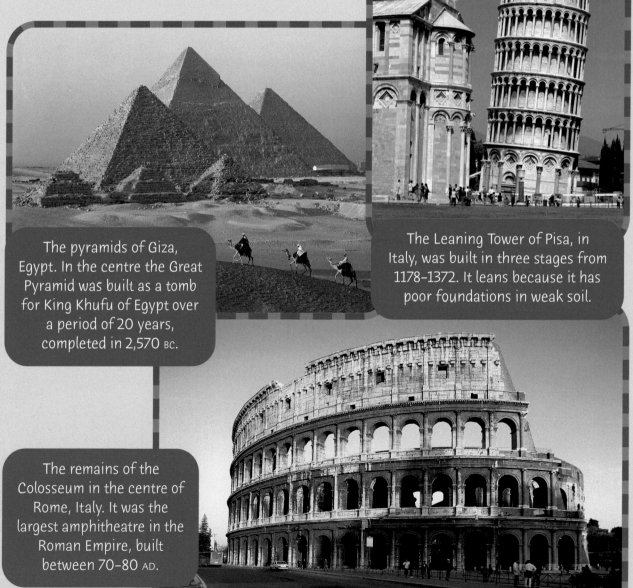

The pyramids of Giza, Egypt. In the centre the Great Pyramid was built as a tomb for King Khufu of Egypt over a period of 20 years, completed in 2,570 BC.

The Leaning Tower of Pisa, in Italy, was built in three stages from 1178–1372. It leans because it has poor foundations in weak soil.

The remains of the Colosseum in the centre of Rome, Italy. It was the largest amphitheatre in the Roman Empire, built between 70–80 AD.

The Taj Mahal, near Agra in India, was built by Shah Jahan between 1632–53 as a memorial to his wife.

The Crystal Palace was originally built in Hyde Park, London, UK, for the Great Exhibition of 1851. It was moved to Sydenham Hill in South London.

One of the most extreme modern examples is the Hundertwasser House in Vienna, Austria, containing the usual offices and apartments … with trees growing out of the rooms! It also has a grass roof, uneven floors and a patchwork of wild colours on the outside. The building attracts visitors from all around the world.

The Guggenheim Museum in Bilbao, Spain, is dedicated to modern art, so the designers wanted an eye-catching building in which to put it. The architect Frank Gehry produced a ship-like design of curved metal and glass which catches and reflects the light.

Did you know?

The designer Friedensreich Hundertwasser loved the building in Vienna, Austria, so much that he refused to accept payment for his work.

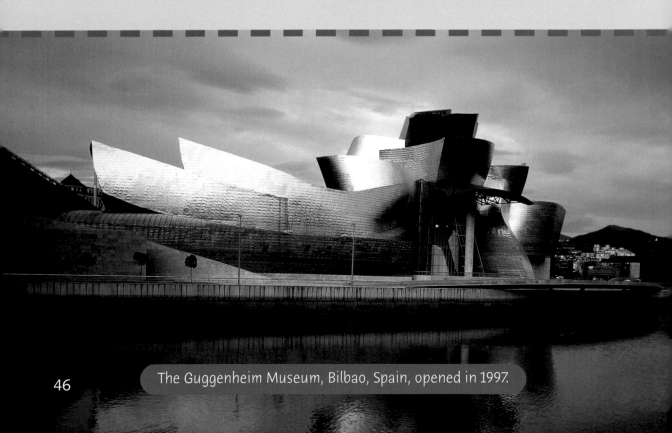

The Guggenheim Museum, Bilbao, Spain, opened in 1997.

The world contains many beautiful places of worship – one spectacular example is the Sagrada Família (Holy Family) cathedral in Barcelona. Designed by Antoni Gaudí, building began in 1883, but the cathedral was still not finished when Gaudí died in 1926. Usually architects try to keep to one building style, but Gaudí's masterpiece is a **mishmash** of several different styles.

the Sagrada Família cathedral, Barcelona, Spain

47

If you're going to design an artistic building, then what better to choose than an art gallery? One of the most famous galleries in the world, the Louvre in Paris, caused a stir in 1989 when it introduced a modern glass pyramid to stand outside its traditional design. The glass allows light to flow into the below-ground entrance hall, as well as giving a superb view of the sky for those inside. Some people love the contrast between the new pyramid and the old gallery, while others think it's a blot on the landscape.

the glass pyramid entrance, the Louvre, Paris, France

Some architects take existing buildings and change their purpose. The Tate Modern art gallery in London used to be a power station. Visitors' jaws drop as they enter the building, stunned by the vast open space of the old **Turbine** Hall.

The American artist Gordon Matta-Clark took unused buildings and cut them open. Slicing houses in half allowed passers-by to inspect the innards of the building. The idea was to create a mix of architecture and archaeology designed to make people think more deeply about their environment.

If you wander around any modern city, in amongst the buildings you'll find statues of all shapes and sizes.

the Turbine Hall, Tate Modern, London, UK

Statues are designed with many different purposes: to make the **cityscape** more beautiful, to impress, to inspire, to surprise you, or maybe to make you laugh.

a statue of a **paparazzo** taking a photograph, Bratislava, Slovak Republic

49

Future designs

So, what will come next? As we've seen, building designs have changed constantly for hundreds of years. It seems likely that they'll carry on changing in the future.

Architects are already starting to build houses that are more friendly to the environment around them. They try to:

- make the house blend in with the landscape
- use solar or wind power to produce the house's energy
- let more sunlight in, rather than relying on electric lighting
- use natural materials such as wood for the outside of the house
- use recycled materials for the walls and insulation.

These building blocks are as strong as concrete, but are actually made out of recycled waste such as glass, paper and sewage.

This house has been built into the ground, so the only visible part is the glass front. The rock and soil around it keep the temperature constant, and the only heating it needs is supplied by the Sun.

For huge events such as the Olympic Games, accommodation needs to be built for up to 20,000 athletes and officials. The Games last just two weeks, so clearly it would be a terrible waste for this Olympic Village to be knocked down afterwards. Designers have to plan the project with the future in mind. Open spaces and parks are included and after the Games the buildings may be converted into homes and schools.

Some architects have even grander designs in mind and are planning complete indoor towns, where a whole community can live without going outdoors! The British architect Norman Foster is the designer of Crystal Island, due to be built in Moscow, Russia. It would become the world's biggest building, containing 900 apartments, 3,000 hotel rooms, a school, cinemas, a theatre, shops and a sports complex. Energy will mostly come from solar panels and wind turbines.

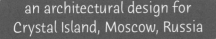
an architectural design for Crystal Island, Moscow, Russia

Maybe you will be one of the designers who will shape the way we live in the next 50 years! If so, one day you may be planning buildings for people to live in on the Moon, or even Mars …

Glossary

architectural   describing a construction which is planned or built by an architect

cityscape   the landscape of a city

foundations   the underground construction that distributes a building's weight so that it does not collapse

gramophones   old-fashioned machines for playing records

hi-tech   short for high-technology

insulation   keeping in the heat by using a thick layer of special material

mishmash   a confused collection or mixture of styles

low-rise   a building with only a few storeys

nomadic   travelling from place to place, especially to find fresh pastures for grazing animals or for hunting

paparazzo   a freelance photographer who takes photos of famous people without their permission

road rage   sudden violent anger that one motorist feels against the actions of another motorist

sat nav   short for satellite navigation, an in-car system that gets its information from satellites, then tells you which way to go

suburbs   areas of housing on the outskirts of large towns and cities

turbine   a machine which produces continuous power, as a result of a wheel or rotor being made to revolve by fast-flowing materials such as water or steam

Victorian   the period of time when Queen Victoria reigned, 1819–1901

Index

how we spend our leisure time

where we eat

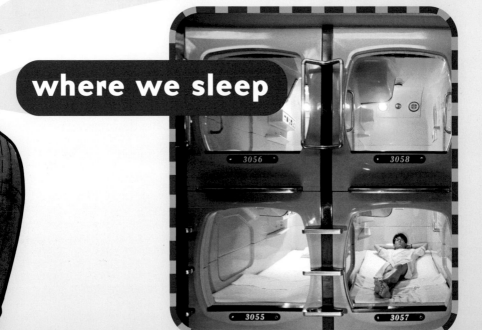

where we sleep

55

Ideas for reading

Written by Clare Dowdall, PhD
Lecturer and Primary Literacy Consultant

Learning objectives: appraise a text quickly, deciding on its value, quality or usefulness; sustain engagement with longer texts using different techniques to make the text come alive; use the techniques of dialogic talk to explore ideas, topics or issues

Curriculum links: Design and Technology: Shelters

Interest words: architectural, cityscape, foundations, hi-tech, insulation, mishmash, low-rise, nomadic, suburbs, turbine

Resources: ICT, reference books, whiteboard/notebooks for listing ideas, images of local buildings and spaces

Getting started

This book can be read over two or more guided reading sessions.

- Look at the front cover together. Ask children what they think the building is (*Burj Al Arab hotel in Dubai*).

- Read the blurb on the back cover together. Create a list of interesting local buildings, spaces and places that the children are familiar with. Discuss the types of decisions that the designers of these places might have had to make.

- Ask children to read the contents. Discuss which chapter headings appeal most and why.

- Skim through the book in pairs, looking for features and sections that seem particularly interesting. Share ideas about how the author makes the book appealing and the information accessible, e.g. *use of vivid images, concise fact boxes, diagrams, "Did you know?" challenges.*

Reading and responding

- Ask children to read pp2–3 independently. Discuss the examples of enduring designs that are featured. Ask children to suggest cars, toys, clothing and sweets that currently have popular designs. Discuss why the designs are popular.

- Read pp4–7 as a group, inviting volunteers to read aloud.